MW00749250

A STUDY OF PSALM 23

by

KRISTIN SCHMUCKER

STUDY CONTRIBUTORS

Designer:
MICHELE YATES

Editor:
MELISSA DENNIS

Contributing Author:
SARAH MORRISON

www.thedailygraceco.com

Unless otherwise noted all Scripture has been taken from the Christian Standard Bible®, Copyright © 2017 by Holman Bible Publishers.
Used by permission. Christian Standard Bible® and CSB® are federally registered trademarks of Holman Bible Publishers.

Designed in the United States of America and printed in China.

Intro

This psalm is one of the most well known portions in all of Scripture. We must be careful not to allow its familiarity to lessen its beauty. It's fame is well deserved, and this psalm has brought comfort and hope to many believers in many different circumstances. This psalm of David is written from the perspective of a shepherd, though David would identify himself as one of the sheep of our Good Shepherd. We can identify with this psalm as followers of Jesus.

There are eight days of devotionals for this psalm. In addition, it is suggested that before beginning, you take a day to read and write out the entirety of the psalm. Do this slowly and take time to meditate on the truth found here. After you have studied through the passage, take another day to write out the psalm again, as well as to write a paraphrase of the psalm in your own words.

There is so much truth to be gleaned from this psalm, and memorizing it is an amazing endeavor. If you take the time to hide these words in your heart, they will be a comfort to you often. Take time to either memorize the entire psalm or choose a verse that is particularly meaningful to memorize before the conclusion of the study.

Week
ONE

READ
Psalm 23

WEEK ONE
DAY ONE

Read + Write

READ ALL OF PSALM 23 AND WRITE IT OUT ON THESE PAGES

_____

_____

_____

_____

_____

_____

_____

_____

_____

_____

_____

_____

_____

_____

_____

_____

_____

PARAPHRASE
Psalm 23

WEEK ONE
DAY TWO

Read + Paraphrase

READ ALL OF PSALM 23 AND PARAPHRASE IT IN YOUR OWN WORDS

The Lord IS MY Shepherd

WEEK ONE
DAY THREE

Psalm 23:1

The Lord is *my* Shepherd. The great "I am" has chosen to be my Shepherd. He has created me to be His own, and then He has paid the price for my soul on the cross of Calvary. He owns me because He has created me. He has also redeemed me, which means to buy back. He has made me His own prized possession and has chosen to graciously lead me in love. When we went astray like sheep, our Messiah took all of our iniquity on Himself (Isaiah 53:6) so that we could become His own. He is not just *a* shepherd, or even *the* shepherd, but He is *my* Shepherd. I am His, and He is mine.

This concept of God being our Shepherd is not isolated to this famous psalm. The concept is found throughout the Old Testament (Genesis 48:15, Genesis 49:24, Psalm 28:9, Psalm 80:1, Psalm 95:7, Psalm 100:3, Isaiah 40:11, Isaiah 49:10). And in the New Testament Jesus tells us that He is the Good Shepherd—the One who lays down His life for His sheep.

Because the Lord is our Shepherd, we shall not want. This phrase that we shall not want is completely dependent on the truth that the Lord is our Shepherd. In Him we are satisfied. In Jesus, we have all that we need. We have all that we need *in Him*, and there is no need for us to crave anything beside Him. He is our Jehovah-Jireh, the Lord who provides. It is so common for us to seek to fill our lives with things that we think will satisfy. We run to shopping, or food, or alcohol, or even business to try to fill our hearts. But those things will never fill us up. This world and all of its pleasures will never satisfy, but Jesus satisfies the longing soul (Psalm 107:9). Alexander Grose said, "Where Christ reveals himself there is satisfaction in the slenderest portion, and without Christ there is emptiness in the greatest fullness." Jesus is truly all that we need. He is our Provider and our Provision. He is the only One that can satisfy our souls and the only One that can cause us to say that we do not want for anything.

He is our Shepherd and our Guide. He is our Portion and our Provider. The Good Shepherd of our souls is all that we need.

The Lord is my shepherd;
I have what I need.

PSALM 23:1

Think about the role of a shepherd, how they care for their sheep, tend to their flock, how the sheep know their voice, etc. In what ways does this metaphor grow your understanding of who God is and how our relationship with Him should function?

Think about the characteristics of sheep, how they can't fend for themselves, how they aren't particularly clever, and how they *need* a shepherd. In what ways does this metaphor expand your knowledge of our own human condition and the necessity of a relationship with God?

What does it truly mean to not want? Do you find yourself completely satisfied in God?

Waters
OF REST

Psalm 23:2

Our tender Shepherd makes us to lie down in green pastures and tenderly leads us to rivers of rest. Jesus is our Shepherd, and when this world moves in chaos around us, Jesus gently makes us lie down. He tells us to rest in Him, because on our own we are so prone to continue to do things in our own strength. He knows exactly what we need and exactly when we need it. We can trust that He is always working for our good. He lies us down and promises us that we are secure in Him (Psalm 4:8). Ezekiel 34:15-16 echoes the truth of this verse as well when it tells us that the Lord Himself will be our Shepherd and that He Himself will make us lie down. He is the one that brings peace and security to our hearts no matter what circumstances this life may bring. We can rest and lie down because we know that He is ours and He is with us.

He leads us to green pastures. He takes us exactly where we need to be. He knows that on our own we may not choose the best things. We are easily distracted by the world around us, but He leads us to the green pastures that He has prepared for us. He places us in the land that is good for us. We may not always understand His plan, but we can trust that He is bringing us to a good place.

Not only does He tenderly make us lie down in green pastures, but He leads us beside still waters. The Hebrew in this verse literally means "waters of rest." He brings us to a place of rest and refreshment. Not just the kind of rest like a good night's sleep, but the kind of rest that rejuvenates our soul. He does not just command us to go there, but He leads us there with Him. Jesus has walked this road before us, and now He leads us to the sweet peace and rest that only He can give. We know that Jesus Himself is the Living Water and the satisfaction of our soul (John 4). Jeremiah 2:13 tells us how easy it is for God's people to neglect the Living Water and to try to make their own cisterns. But the water we try to create for ourselves will never satisfy—only Jesus satisfies. We find sweet rest in Jesus alone.

"Thou hast made us for thyself, O Lord, and our heart is restless until it finds its rest in thee." – Augustine of Hippo

---

He lets me lie down in green pastures; he leads me beside quiet waters.

PSALM 23:2

Pay attention to the verbs "lets" and "leads." What does this tell you about the sheep-shepherd relationship? Spend some time in self-examination. Do you submit to God's leadership in your life?

Think about the symbolism and meaning of "green pastures" and "still waters." How does this verse remind you of the life-giving nature of a relationship with God?

In what ways does this verse reinforce to you that God will provide rest for us? Do you trust in His faithfulness to provide reprieve for you?

He Restores
MY SOUL

Psalm 23:3

"When the soul grows sorrowful he revives it; when it is sinful he sanctifies it; when it is weak he strengthens it." – Charles Spurgeon

After resting in the Savior and being filled with the still water, David says that the believer's soul is restored. The presence of God has power to restore all who come to Him. He is always waiting to restore and standing with arms open wide to bring us close to Him.

The Hebrew word often translated as "restore" or "renew" shows us the many things that our God does when He restores our soul. He revives us and draws us back to Himself. Tucked in the Gesenius Hebrew-Chaldee Lexicon for this verse is the word "refresh." Our souls are renewed when the Lord refreshes us. He uses that still water from verse 2 to bring refreshment to our weary souls. We are refreshed with the water of His Word each day as we come to Scripture and seek the Living Water Himself (John 4).

Psalm 19:7 tells us that, "The law of the Lord is perfect, reviving the soul." The word in this verse for "revive" is the word *shuwb*, and it is the same Hebrew word that is used for "restore" in Psalm 23:3. This shows us again how God uses His Word to renew, revive, and refresh our weary souls. His word is living, and it also gives us life.

David had been through many different circumstances in His life. He had faced much suffering and hardship, but as he reflected back on his life he saw the truth that God does not have to change our circumstances to refresh and restore us. He doesn't have to change my circumstances to give me peace; I have peace because He is with me.

With our God, there is refreshment for our souls and streams of water—even in the desert. This is how our God works. He brings restoration and refreshment even in the desert times of this life. We can be confident and sure that our God will refresh our soul in the wilderness and restore us to Himself. He is always working on our behalf as our loving Shepherd to guide us, lead us, refresh us, and give us everything that we need to follow Him.

Look, I am about to do something new; even now it is coming. Do you not see it? Indeed, I will make a way in the wilderness, rivers in the desert.
- Isaiah 43:19

He renews my life

PSALM 23:3a

Take a moment to look up a definition of the word "restore." In what ways does this definition help you to engage with this verse better? Does knowing the full definition grow your understanding of God's care for us?

What other instances in the Bible can you think of where God has brought about restoration? How do these examples and accounts of restoration give you encouragement that God will be faithful to restore and refresh you?

Are there particular things in your life that you're waiting on God to restore? Spend some time in prayer, asking that God would bring about restoration according to His purposes and grow your relationship with Him in the process.

The Lord is my shepherd;
I have what I need.
He lets me lie down in green pastures;
he leads me beside quiet waters.
He renews my life;
he leads me along the right paths
for his name's sake.
Even when I go through the darkest valley,
I fear no danger,
for you are with me;
your rod and your staff—they comfort me.

You prepare a table before me
in the presence of my enemies;
you anoint my head with oil;
my cup overflows.
Only goodness and faithful love will pursue me
all the days of my life,
and I will dwell in the house of the Lord
as long as I live.

Psalm 23

Week One Notes

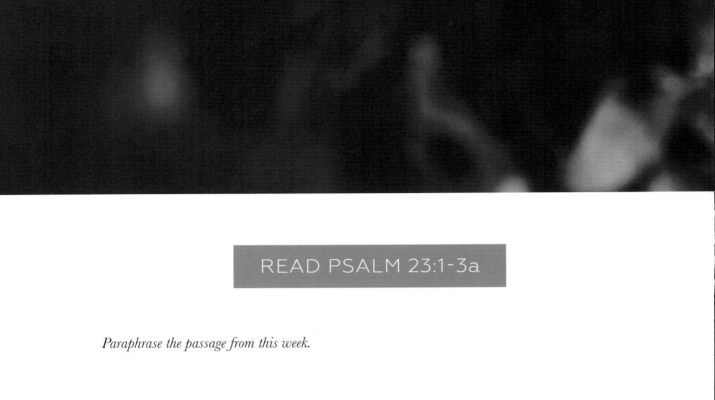

Paraphrase the passage from this week.

What did you observe from this week's text about God and His character?

What does the passage teach about the condition of mankind and about yourself?

How does this passage point to the gospel?

How should you respond to this passage? What is the personal application?

What specific action steps can you take this week to apply the passage?

Week

TWO

HE

leads

ME

WEEK TWO
DAY ONE

Psalm 23:3

Again we are reminded that He leads us. He leads us in paths of righteousness for His name's sake. David Guzik says that, "The sheep didn't need to know where the green pastures or still waters were; all he needed to know was where the shepherd was." What a comfort to know that we do not need to know everything about our life. We can rest secure under the leadership and guidance of our Shepherd who will show us exactly the way that we should go. He will lead us.

We can be confident that our Good Shepherd will lead us in the paths that He has already laid out before us. He knows the way that we are taking, and He has prepared it before us. He has sovereignly prepared this path for us, and He will lead us to the chosen destination. The temptation for us is to go our own way just like sheep do (Isaiah 53:6). We don't always want to trust that His paths are good and right. We think we might know a better way. So often we would much rather rush ahead rather than follow our Shepherd. But God's ways are always the best ways. We can trust Him! As we lean into Him and stop leaning on our own finite understanding, He will direct our paths and lead us in the way of righteousness (Proverbs 3:5-6).

He will lead us in the way that we should go for the glory and praise of His name. His name is all of His Word and His character, and when

He leads us it will display for all to see the beauty and truth of who He is. Our lives become witnesses to the majesty of His name as we proclaim to others that He is good, that He has been good to us, and that He can do the same for them. What a privilege to let our lights shine for our Shepherd and King. What an honor to be led by Him.

---

he leads me along the right paths for his name's sake.

PSALM 23:3b

Meditate on the quote from David Guzik in today's devotion. What are some practical ways in which you can know where the Shepherd is?

Look up the definition to "righteousness" and then think about what exactly the "right paths" are. Why do you think righteousness is important in our relationship with God?

Think about the phrase "for His name's sake." In what ways does this verse grow your understanding of the purpose of our witness to the world? Does this verse give you encouragement to continue to grow and live a holy life?

YOU ARE
With Me

WEEK TWO
DAY TWO

Psalm 23:4

It is no secret that this life is full of joy, but it is also mingled with sorrow. Even the strongest believer will face seasons of difficulty and hardship, but even still we have nothing to fear because our God is with us. Here the tone of the psalm shifts, and suddenly David goes to speaking about his Shepherd to speaking to Him. What a sacred privilege that we can speak to our God. No matter what season of life we may be facing, we can speak to the One who is in control.

In life there are mountaintops and there are valleys. We like the mountaintops, but we tend to despise the valleys. The psalmist reminds us though, that we do not need to fear these valleys because the Lord is with us even there. We can face any valley knowing that He is with us and that He will use even the darkest and deepest valley for our good.

We do not walk through the valley of death, but only the valley of the shadow of death. Our Jesus has conquered death, and Charles Spurgeon says that, "only the shadow of it remains." Spurgeon points out that "Nobody is afraid of a shadow, for a shadow cannot stop a man's pathway even for a moment. The shadow of a dog cannot bite; the shadow of a sword cannot kill; the shadow of death cannot destroy us." We do not need to fear the valley of the shadow of death or any other valley this life may bring, because our Shepherd is with us and leading us right to where we need to be.

This world is full of evil—this much is true. But with our God, we have no need to fear it. Our God is stronger than anything that could ever come against us. In our moments of fear, we can call upon the name of our God who will soothe every worry and calm every fear with His presence. He is with us. He is with us in the valley and He is with us on the mountaintop, and because of His presence there is *nothing* that we need to fear.

Even when I go through the darkest valley, I fear no danger, for you are with me

PSALM 23:4a

How can the knowledge that the trials we suffer through are but a *shadow* strengthen you to walk wisely and joyfully despite pain?

"I fear no danger" sounds like a pretty lofty statement. How does it comfort you to know that there is no need to fear because of the presence of the Lord in our lives?

Spend some time in prayer, praising God for always being with you and asking that He would cast out the fears that remain in you.

THEY *Comfort* ME

WEEK TWO
DAY THREE

Psalm 23:4

We find comfort in the valley and everyday with our God. His rod and His staff remind us that He is all powerful and that He will guide us and correct us so that we will go the way we ought to go. We can be comforted by the truth that because He is in charge, we don't have to try to be.

The rod is used by a shepherd to ward off enemies, to count the sheep, and to examine each one closely, correcting wayward sheep along the way. In the same way, our God fights off our enemies while also examining our hearts and correcting us when we wander from Him. It is a comfort to be protected from outside danger by our God as well as corrected of the danger that takes up residence in our hearts that are so prone to wandering from the fold. Conviction should be sweet to the believer. It is a reminder that we are His, and it is an invitation to restoration. We find protection, security, and comfort in our Shepherd's rod.

The staff is the symbolic mark of a shepherd, and it is this instrument that is used again and again to rescue the sheep from the danger they wander into and to bring them near to the shepherd himself. In the same way, our Good Shepherd brings us near to Himself any time we have wandered or found ourselves in danger. Our Savior gently pulls us back to Himself again and again. He protects us from every danger and rescues us. As the shepherd uses his staff to gently tap and prod the side of the sheep to show them the way that they should go, so our Shepherd and Savior gently nudges us with His Holy Spirit to lead us in the way that we should go. What sweet comforts are the rod and the staff of our Shepherd to us!

your rod and your staff—
they comfort me.

PSALM 23:4b

Think about the role of the shepherd's rod. Do you find ease that God, as our Shepherd, provides conviction and protection simultaneously?

Think about the role of the shepherd's staff. How does its function differ from that of the rod? Why do you think this is important?

Meditate on the comfort talked about in this verse—David's comfort was not only in the protection and security found in his Shepherd, but also in the conviction and correction. What does this tell you about loving the Lord's instruction for us? How does this encourage you to pursue Him more?

YOU *prepare* A TABLE

WEEK TWO
DAY FOUR

Psalm 23:5

In the presence of our great Shepherd there is peace and joy even in the most difficult of seasons and situations. Our Shepherd prepares a table for us. It is set out with extreme care and prepared—not hastily thrown together. Our Savior gives His very best to prepare this great banquet for us. The One who has guided and protected us and brought us to this place will also rejoice with us and celebrate at this great banquet. The life of the believer should be one characterized by great joy. How could we not be filled with *joy* after all our God has done for us?

There is some discussion over whether this table refers to a table for eating or to a plain of land that was often referred to as a table during this time period. Though we cannot be sure the exact meaning, the implication is the same either way that our God has prepared a place of joy and rest and rejoicing for the people that He loves.

The next words catch us off guard if we will not be blinded by our familiarity with this passage. This table that He has prepared for us—it is in the presence of our enemies. The enemies have not disappeared, but because of who our God is, we can rest and rejoice and have peace and joy right in the presence of our enemies. Our joy is not dependent on our circumstances but on our Savior. He pours out fresh anointing on His people and fills their cup to overflowing.

There is so much joy to be found in our Shepherd. So we can eat and we can overflow with joy right in the midst of the struggles of this life because we know that our God is greater than anything that we may face in this life.

You prepare a table before me in the presence of my enemies; you anoint my head with oil; my cup overflows.

PSALM 23:5

Notice the verb "prepare" in this verse. Why do you think it might be significant for us to understand the Lord *prepares* a table before us?

How does the line "in the presence of my enemies" illustrate to you that God is attentive to justice?

In the second half of this verse we see the phrase, "my cup overflows." How does this symbol of abundance point back to the concept portrayed in the green pastures and still waters in verse 2?

Only
GOODNESS
AND MERCY

WEEK TWO
DAY FIVE

Psalm 23:6

Surely goodness and mercy shall follow me. The word here for "surely" literally means *only*. Someday, I will look back on my life and I will see only the goodness and steadfast love of my God. Certainly there were trials along the way, but when I gaze at my life from His perspective suddenly things will become much clearer. I will see that He had a plan all along. I did not understand it fully in the moment, but on that day I will see clearly His grace and mercy on my life. I will see that even the things that felt bad and hard were good for me. In His grace, He allows me to walk through this life exactly where He has placed me, because He knows that it is good for me. His ways are *only* good toward me.

He was not just good on the easy and happy days, but all the days of my life. Every moment was an overflow of His love and care as my tender Shepherd. As He called me His own and promised all I would need, He was good. As He made me lie down and led me to waters of rest, He was good. As He restored my soul and prepared my path, He was good. As He walked beside me through the valley of the shadow of death, He was good. As He comforted me with His rod and staff, He was good. As He prepared a table for me and gave me joy in the presence of my enemies, He was good. On every day and in every way, He was good. The darkest day of my life is still overcome with the bright light of His goodness and steadfast love for me. His mercy here is His *Hesed* love. The love that will not let me go. The love that pursues me and keeps covenant. The love that we cannot find words to express.

Someday we will spend our eternity in His presence, and we will worship Him for who He is and all that He has done for us. On that day we will look back and see not our trials, but His faithfulness. We will see only His goodness and mercy. But for now, we must trust our Shepherd. We must cling to Him and follow His leading. We must trust in faith that even in our trials He is working for our good. We must trust Him that He only deals with us in goodness and steadfast love, and believe that He will use everything we face in this life and everything we face today as an outpouring and overflow of His grace and mercy for us as His own. And someday we will understand. *Every moment of our life is an outpour of His grace.*

What does the word "surely" or "only" convey to you? Does this verse give you confidence and certainty in Christ?

How do we "dwell" in the house of the Lord? In what ways does this verse teach you to abide in God?

Now that we've finished reading through this chapter, think back on what you've learned. In what ways has this study grown your understanding of God? In what ways has this study encouraged you to continue growing in the knowledge and understanding of His word?

Only goodness and faithful love will pursue me all the days of my life, and I will dwell in the house of the Lord as long as I live.

PSALM 23:6

Week Two Notes

READ PSALM 23:3b-6

Paraphrase the passage from this week.

What did you observe from this week's text about God and His character?

What does the passage teach about the condition of mankind and about yourself?

How does this passage point to the gospel?

How should you respond to this passage? What is the personal application?

What specific action steps can you take this week to apply the passage?

Read + Paraphrase

NOW THAT YOU HAVE FINISHED THE STUDY MATERIAL, READ
PSALM 23 AND PARAPHRASE IT IN YOUR OWN WORDS AGAIN

What is the Gospel?

Thank you for reading and enjoying this study with us! We are abundantly grateful for the Word of God, the instruction we glean from it, and the ever-growing understanding about God's character from it. We're also thankful that Scripture continually points to one thing in innumerable ways: the gospel.

We remember our brokenness when we read about the fall of Adam and Eve in the garden of Eden (Genesis 3), when sin entered into a perfect world and maimed it. We remember the necessity that something innocent must die to pay for our sin when we read about the atoning sacrifices in the Old Testament. We read that we have all sinned and fallen short of the glory of God (Romans 3:23), and that the penalty for our brokenness, the wages of our sin, is death (Romans 6:23). We all are in need of grace, mercy, and most importantly—we all need a Savior.

We consider the goodness of God when we realize that He did not plan to leave us in this dire state. We see His promise to buy us back from the clutches of sin and death in Genesis 3:15. And we see that promise accomplished with Jesus Christ on the cross. Jesus Christ knew no sin yet became sin so that we might become righteous through His sacrifice (2 Corinthians 5:21.) Jesus was tempted in every way that we are and lived sinlessly. He was reviled, yet still yielded Himself for our sake, that we may have life abundant in Him. Jesus lived the perfect life that we could not live and died the death that we deserved.

The gospel is profound yet simple. There are many mysteries in it that we can never exhaust this side of heaven, but there is still overwhelming weight to its implications in this life. The gospel is the telling of our sinfulness and God's goodness, and this gracious gift compels a response. We are saved by grace through faith (Ephesians 2:9,) which means that we rest with faith in the grace that Jesus Christ displayed on the cross. We cannot save ourselves from our brokenness or do any amount of good works to merit God's favor, but we can have faith that what Jesus accomplished in His death, burial, and resurrection was more than enough for our salvation and our eternal delight. When we accept God, we are commanded to die to our self and our sinful desires and live a life worthy of the calling we have received (Ephesians 4:1). The gospel compels us to be sanctified, and in so doing, we are conformed to the likeness of Christ Himself.

This is hope. This is redemption. This is the gospel.

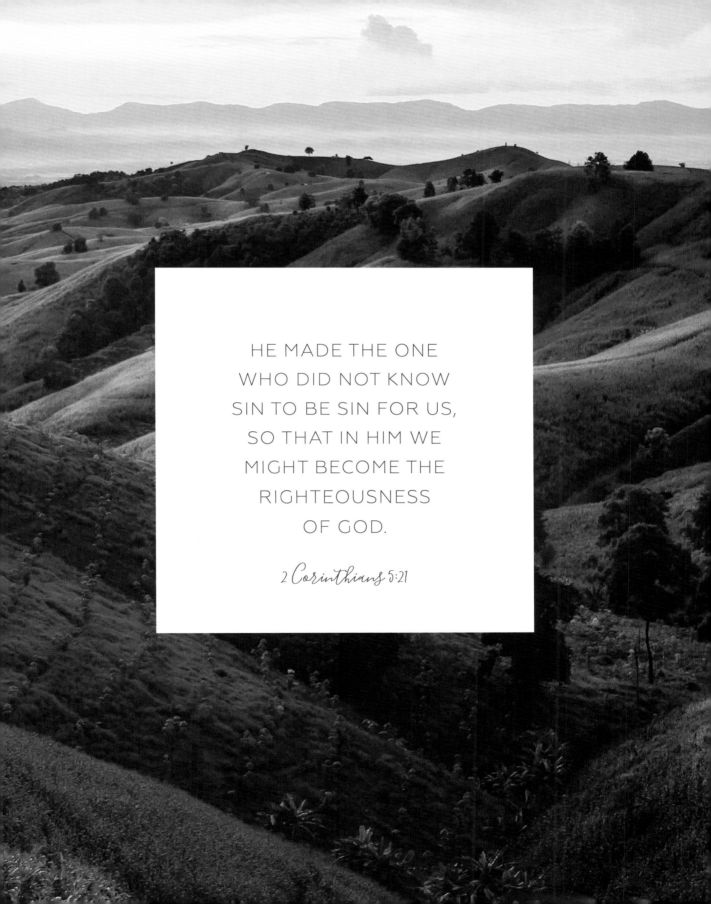

HE MADE THE ONE
WHO DID NOT KNOW
SIN TO BE SIN FOR US,
SO THAT IN HIM WE
MIGHT BECOME THE
RIGHTEOUSNESS
OF GOD.

2 Corinthians 5:21

FOR STUDYING GOD'S
WORD WITH US!

CONNECT WITH US:

@THEDAILYGRACECO

@KRISTINSCHMUCKER

CONTACT US:

INFO@THEDAILYGRACECO.COM

SHARE:

#THEDAILYGRACECO

#LAMPANDLIGHT

WEBSITE:

WWW.THEDAILYGRACECO.COM